The non-fatal offences against the person

(including *actus reus* and *mens rea*)

Part of *The Law Explained* series

Sally Russell LLB (Hons), PGCE

My main objective has been to combine legal accuracy with a style that is accessible to all students, so I hope you will find this book both stimulating and helpful. Fully updated with recent cases and laws it is written in a lively, clear and accessible way and is designed to help students of all learning styles to understand the subject.

Although aimed at A-Level the books provide a good base for 1st Year LLB, ILEX and other courses, and can be used as self-study guides.

Each Chapter contains *examples* to help you see how the law relates to real life situations; *tasks* and *self-test questions*, to help you check your understanding, as well as *examination tips* and **application practice** to help you prepare for problem questions. Where applicable the books also contain **tips and guidance on evaluating** the law to help with essay questions. **Summaries** and **diagrams** help to make the law clear and the **'must-know' cases are highlighted**. Answers are given for the tasks and self-test questions either in the book or on my website at www.drsr.org

The *'the law explained'* series offers a more in-depth coverage of individual areas with additional tasks, examples and examination practice. This means you can pick those topics for which you need more guidance (all the answers are included in the book).

For a range of free interactive exercises please go to www.drsr.org and click on 'Free Exercises' to see what's available.

Other books by Sally Russell

As new books may be available by the time you read this I have not listed my other books by title. They currently include crime and tort at AS level, crime, tort and concepts of law for both the AQA and OCR examination board at A2 level and various books in *'the law explained'* series. For the most up to date list of what is available please check my author's page on Amazon or visit my website at www.drsr.org. All my books are available in both Kindle and paperback format.

About the author

Sally Russell was formerly head of law at a sixth-form college, a senior examiner for AQA and tort advisor for the Institute of Legal Executive Tutorial College. She has written various materials for both teachers and students, for Pearson Education, Hodder education and the National Extension College. She is also a regular contributor to the A-Level Law Review. For more information visit www.drsr.org

I0463578

Table of contents

Actus reus is significant in result crimes, such as ABH, where it must be shown D caused the resulting harm, so the rules on causation are important. *Mens rea* of intent or recklessness is needed for all these offences. The first chapter therefore contains a review of these issues as far as they relate to the non-fatal offences. Don't be tempted to skip this bit even if you studied them for AS. You will have a good base to build on, but you need more depth to your knowledge at this level so concentrate on developing and evaluating what you know.

The tasks are intended to reinforce your learning so do these as you go along. The answers are at the end of the book. Some tasks will just ask you to jot down a few thoughts for use in an essay question, so there are no answers to these, but keep your notes for revision and exam practice. I have included occasional quotes so use these too; they show that you know what judges have to say about the law.

There are also some free interactive exercises at www.drsr.org

The five offences against the person you need to study are commonly called 'the assaults'. However, they are separate and distinct offences, with different rules on each.

The common law offence of assault covers two offences

> assault

> battery

The three statutory offences under the **Offences against the Person Act 1861** are

> **s 47**, assault occasioning actual bodily harm

> **s 20**, grievous bodily harm and wounding

> **s 18**, grievous bodily harm and wounding with intent

We will cover assault and battery in Chapter 2 and go on to the three statutory offences in Chapter 3. There is an overlap between the offences so the revision chapter contains a summary of all the offences with a brief explanation of what is required in each case.

Example

Jane threatens Jenny and then pushes her. Jenny is scared and runs away. She trips and grazes her knee. Frightening Jenny is assault, pushing her is battery. Jenny grazed her knee which is actual bodily harm, **s 47**. If she is seriously hurt or cut badly it will be grievous bodily harm or wounding, **s 20**. If Jane *intended* to harm Jenny seriously, it would be grievous bodily harm or wounding with intent, **s 18**.

Examination tip

Note the date of the Act. It is very old and in need of reform. Reforms have been suggested but not implemented and this is a popular area for evaluation questions. There is a full summary of all the offences together with criticisms and a note of some of the proposed reforms in the revision chapter.

Criminal cases are usually in the form *R v the defendant*. It is acceptable to use just the name so if the case is **R v Miller**, I have called it **Miller**. If another form is used, e.g., **DPP v Miller** I have used the full title, as you may want to look up the case for further information. Civil cases are between the *claimant* and the *defendant*, although you will see the word *'plaintiff'* in cases before 1999.

There is a list of some common abbreviations in the appendix at the end of the booklet.

Actus reus

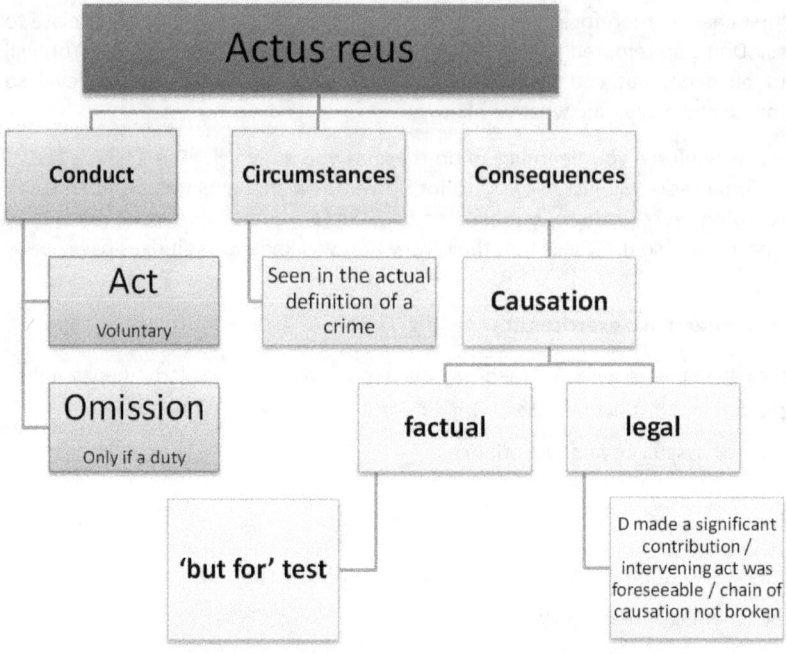

Conduct

In most crimes, the act must be voluntary. This is seen in **Leicester V Pearson 1952**, where a car driver was prosecuted for failing to give precedence to a pedestrian on a zebra crossing. It was shown that his car had been pushed onto the crossing by another car hitting him from behind. He was acquitted because he had not acted voluntarily. This could apply to the non-fatal offences against the person where, e.g., X pushes Y into another person who is injured. It will be X not Y who is liable for the injury because Y did not act voluntarily.

Circumstances

Many crimes are committed only if the conduct is carried out in particular circumstances. An example is battery. A battery is using unlawful force on someone, so that if, for example, D acted in self-defence then in these circumstances the act is lawful. The *actus reus* is not satisfied.

Consequences and causation

Crimes where a particular consequence is part of the *actus reus* are called **result crimes**. For an assault occasioning actual bodily harm (ABH), some kind of harm must result from (be caused by) D's act or omission. For GBH serious harm must result and for wounding there must be a cut through both layers of skin.

The prosecution must prove causation both **factually** and **legally**.

Factual causation is proved using the 'but for' test. For the non-fatal offences the prosecution must show that 'but for' D's conduct, the victim would not have feared harm (assault) incurred unlawful force (battery) been harmed (ABH) been seriously harmed (GBH) or been cut (wounding).

Key case

In **White 1910**, D put cyanide in a drink intending to kill his mother, who was found dead shortly afterwards with the drink 3 parts full. In fact, the mother had died of a heart attack unconnected with the poison. The son was found not guilty of murder. He had the *mens rea* (he intended to kill her) but not the *actus reus* (his act didn't cause her death). He was guilty of attempted murder, however.

Legal causation is based on the 'chain of causation'. There must be an unbroken link, or chain, between D's action and the result. When something has occurred after D's original act, then it may be argued that the chain of causation is broken.

Key case

In **Cheshire 1991**, due to negligent treatment by the hospital, the victim of a shooting died. The court held that as long as D's action was a **'significant and operative'** cause of the result (in this case a death) it need not be the sole cause. Hospital treatment will not break the chain unless it is "*so independent of D's acts and in itself so potent in causing death, that the contribution made by D is insignificant.*" Thus if D makes a significant contribution to the result this is enough, even if there are other causes as well.

In **Pagett 1983**, D fired a shotgun at armed police while holding a girl hostage in front of him. They returned fire, killing the girl. The court held that the actions of the police did not break the chain because shooting back was a 'natural consequence' of his having shot first. This is based on the principle from **Roberts 1971**, that a foreseeable act does not break the chain.

Key Case

In **Roberts 1971**, D committed an assault on a girl by trying to take off her coat while in a moving car. She jumped out and was injured. He was charged with actual bodily harm. The court had to decide whether the assault caused the injury, or whether her actions broke the chain of causation. It was held that only if it was something that no reasonable person could foresee would the chain of causation be broken by the victim's actions. Here this was not the case so he was liable for her injuries. This means a magistrate or jury may take into account that the victim may do the wrong thing in the agony of the moment.

In **Pagett**, it was the act of a third party (the police) that was foreseeable. In **Roberts,** the act of the victim was foreseeable and so did not break the chain of causation between the assault and the injury she incurred when jumping out of the car.

A final point, it was recognised in **Roberts** that V might do the wrong thing in the agony of the moment. However, in **Williams & Davis 1992**, the CA said that if V does something "*so daft or unexpected*" that no reasonable person could be expected to foresee it, the chain of causation would be broken.

Examination tip

It may be difficult to decide what acts should be considered 'independent' or 'potent' enough to break the causation chain or what amounts to a 'daft' act by the victim. There can be a thin line between doing 'something wrong in the agony of the moment' and doing something 'daft'. The main thing is to be logical. State the law from **Cheshire** and **Roberts** on these issues and apply it to the facts given. If someone does something that causes harm which seems independent of D's act, or the victim does something wholly unpredictable, then go on to say that this could break the chain of causation so that D is not liable.

Coincidence of *actus reus* and *mens rea*

Although *actus reus* and *mens rea* must coincide, the court may view the *actus reus* as continuing. In **Fagan v Metropolitan Police Commissioner 1969**, D accidentally drove onto a police officer's foot whilst parking. He didn't move his car when asked to, and was convicted of assaulting a police officer in the execution of his duty. He argued that there was no *mens rea* at the time of the act (driving onto his foot). The court held that there was a continuing act. This started with driving onto the police officer's foot and continued up to the refusal to move. Thus, not moving when asked to was part of the original act (a battery) and at this time, he did have *mens rea*.

In **Thabo Meli 1954**, the Ds tried to kill a man and rolled his body over a cliff. As it happened, he wasn't dead and the actual cause of death was exposure. The Ds argued that the first act (the attack), although done with *mens rea,* was not the cause of death (so no *actus reus*). The second act (pushing him over the cliff) was the cause of death, but was not accompanied by *mens rea* as they thought he was already dead. The court said that it was "*impossible to divide up what was really one series of acts in this way*".

The 'thin skull' rule

The chain is not broken by a particular vulnerability in the victim. Lawton LJ said in **Blaue 1975**, "*those who use violence on other people must take their victims as they find them*". Also known as the 'thin-skull rule', it means that if a particular disability in the victim makes them more likely to die, D is still liable. The 'disability' is usually physical (like a pre-existing medical condition such as a 'thin skull') but in **Blaue** it was the fact that she was a Jehovah's Witness and so refused to have a blood transfusion.

Examination tip

In a problem question, look out for anything that D can argue broke the chain. For example, D attacks someone and, as they are running away, they are hit by a bike. **Roberts** can be used to say that this is unlikely to break the chain. Look out for words like 'near the road'. This suggests harm is foreseeable. If V refuses treatment, you may need the 'thin-skull' rule. Here look out for the reason. If it is a 'daft' decision, then **Blaue** may be distinguished and **Williams & Davis 1992** followed. If it is due to religious beliefs, **Blaue** will be followed.

Mens rea

The two main types of *mens rea* are intention and recklessness. We will review these briefly and then look at the specific issues of *mens rea* as they apply to the offences themselves in the next two chapters.

Direct Intent

Direct intent means the result is D's aim or purpose. This is what most of us would understand by intention. If you pick up a loaded gun and fire it at someone with the aim of killing them, it can be said without any difficulty that you intended to do so. Intention was defined in **Mohan 1975** as 'the decision to bring about' the result, or prohibited consequence, whether that result was desired or not. The courts have given the concept of intention a wider meaning, however. This is referred to as oblique, or indirect, intent.

Oblique or indirect intent

Here the consequence isn't D's aim but is 'virtually certain' to occur because of D's actions.

The law on oblique intent was clarified somewhat by the HL in **Woollin 1998**, which confirmed the standard direction for the jury given by the CA in **Nedrick 1986**. This was:

> That death or serious bodily harm was a **virtual certainty** as a result of the defendant's actions and
>
> **the defendant appreciated** that such was the case

Recklessness

Subjective recklessness is used for most crimes as an alternative *mens rea* to intent.

Key case

Cunningham 1957 provides the test for subjective recklessness. D ripped a gas meter from a basement wall in order to steal the money in the meter. Gas escaped and seeped through to an adjoining property where an occupant was overcome by the fumes. D was charged with maliciously administering a noxious substance, and argued that he did not realise the risk of gas escaping. The CA quashed his conviction having interpreted 'maliciously' to mean with subjective recklessness. The prosecution had failed to prove that D was aware that his actions might cause harm. The test for subjective recklessness is therefore that:

D is aware of the existence of a risk (of the consequence occurring) and deliberately goes ahead and takes that risk.

There were two types of recklessness but objective recklessness (which came from **Caldwell**) is now abolished. Subjective means looking at what was in the *defendant's* mind.

Key case

In **Gemmell and Richards 2003**, two boys aged 11 and 13 set light to some papers outside the back of a shop. Several premises were badly damaged. They were convicted of arson based on objective recklessness, i.e., that the risk of damage was obvious to a reasonable person. Their ages were therefore not taken into account. Their appeal went to the HL, which used the **1966 Practice Statement** to overrule its previous decision in **Caldwell**. The *mens rea* for all crimes requiring recklessness is now subjective (**Cunningham**) recklessness, so that the *defendant* must recognise that there is a risk, of e.g., the resulting harm.

Examination tip

When applying the law on intent you need only use **Nedrick** and **Woollin**, and only then in cases of oblique intent, not where it is direct. This was made clear in **Woollin**. D's knowledge will be an important factor. Look carefully at the facts for information such as 'they knew that ...' or 'unknown to them ...'. These comments will help you to decide whether intent is direct or indirect and to apply the test if necessary to conclude whether there is intent at all. If applying the law on recklessness you only need to discuss subjective (**Cunningham**) recklessness. This is now the law as confirmed by the HL in **Gemmell**.

Transferred Malice

Mens rea can be transferred from the intended victim to the actual victim. This means that if you intend to hit Steve but miss and hit Joe you cannot say 'but I didn't intend to hit Joe so I had no *mens rea*'. In **Latimer 1886**, D aimed a blow at X with his belt but missed and seriously wounded V. He had the intent (*mens rea*) to hit X, and this intent was transferred to the wounding (*actus reus*) of V. Thus, he had both the *mens rea* and the *actus reus* of wounding. However, the *actus reus* and *mens rea* must be for the *same* crime so if you throw a stone at a window but hit a person the *mens rea* of intending to damage the window cannot be transferred to the *actus reus* of a non-fatal offence against the person.

For some free interactive exercises visit www.drsr.org and click on Free Exercises to see what's available.

Common assault: Assault and Battery

Common assault includes two separate offences, assault and battery. It is called common assault because it comes from the common law. This means that assault and battery are not defined in any statute so the rules come from cases. The **Criminal Justice Act 1988 s 39** classifies them as summary offences (triable only in the magistrates' court) so for convenience they are charged under this section.

Examination tip

It is better not to say they are *offences* under **s 39 Criminal Justice Act**. They are common law offences *charged* under the **Act**. Think of common assault as an umbrella under which the two crimes of assault and battery sit. They frequently occur together. If you need to discuss both, then refer to common assault and then describe assault and battery in turn.

The definitions as developed by case law are currently:

Assault: to cause someone to apprehend immediate and unlawful personal violence

Battery: the unlawful application of force to another

Remember that all parts of the *actus reus* must be proved for all crimes.

Examples

Matt threatens to hit Leon, who is scared. This is an assault because Leon 'apprehends', or fears, immediate violence.

Matt threatens to hit Leon if he ever sees him in the area again. Even if Leon is in fear of violence, he is not in fear of *immediate* violence. Part of the *actus reus* is missing, so there is no assault

Matt hits Leon. This is battery as Matt has used unlawful force (there is no need for any injury or harm to result)

Matt taps Leon on the shoulder to attract his attention. Even though he has applied force, it is *lawful* force, because there is implied consent to this type of touching. Part of the *actus reus* is missing, so there is no battery

Matt threatens to hit Leon and then does so. Here there is both an assault and a battery.

Matt hits Leon from behind. Here there is a battery but no assault because Leon cannot be in fear of violence if he doesn't see it coming.

Assault

The definition of assault is 'an act by which a person **intentionally or recklessly causes another to apprehend immediate and unlawful violence**'. As the law comes from cases, you may see slightly different definitions in other cases. This definition was used by the CA in **Ireland 1996** (discussed below) and confirmed by the HL the following year, in the twin appeals of **Ireland & Burstow 1997**.

cause another to apprehend

In simple terms apprehend means fear. It is the effect on the victim that is important with assault. Assault is not the actual violence but the threat of it which puts V in fear of violence.

Examples

D walks into a bank pointing a banana concealed in a bag and saying, "I have a gun. Give me the money or I'll shoot you." The cashier is very frightened and does as D says. This is an assault. The fact that there is no possibility of carrying out the threat doesn't matter. V is in fear of immediate violence.

D walks into a bank pointing a real gun and saying, "Give me the money or I'll shoot." The cashier knows him from college and she thinks he is doing it as a joke. This is unlikely to be assault. D has *mens rea* but not *actus reus*, because V doesn't believe that any violence is about to take place.

Whether it amounts to assault therefore depends on whether or not V thinks that violence is about to take place (and so is in fear of it).

Early cases indicated that words would not amount to assault unless accompanied by some threatening gesture (like raising your fist). This is no longer the case

Key case

In **Ireland**, D had repeatedly made silent telephone calls, accompanied by heavy breathing, to three women who then suffered psychiatric illness. In the appeal to the HL in 1997, Lord Steyn confirmed that words would be enough for assault, saying,

> "The proposition that a gesture may amount to an assault, but that words can never suffice, is unrealistic and indefensible. A thing said is also a thing done. There is no reason why something said should be incapable of causing an apprehension of immediate personal violence, e.g., a man accosting a woman in a dark alley saying 'come with me or I will stab you.' I would, therefore, reject the proposition that an assault can never be committed by words".

In **Constanza 1997**, a case of stalking, the CA also held that words alone could amount to an assault. In **Smith v Chief Superintendent of Woking Police Station 1983**, a 'peeping Tom' assaulted a woman by looking at her through her bedroom window at night. This was held to be an assault as he had caused her to be frightened.

Therefore, it is clear that words, or even silence, can now amount to an assault.

Essay pointer

As we saw, whether the victim is in fear is the important question. It therefore seems right that words, or even silence, should amount to assault if they put the victim in fear of violence. The law has arguably become more satisfactory over the years, at least on this point.

Words may prevent an assault

If D accompanies the threat with words which indicate that no violence will take place then there is no assault. An example of this is seen in a very old case. In **Turbeville v Savage 1669**, D was having an argument with V and placed his hand on the hilt of his sword. This would indicate an assault. He then said 'If it were not assize time, I would not take such language from you'. There was held to be no assault. The statement was held to indicate that he would *not* assault V because it was assize time and the judges were in town.

Examples

Almost all situations where the word 'if' is included in the threat will indicate that an assault will not take place except in certain circumstances

If you were younger, I would beat you up

If you hurt my sister, I will hit you

If I hadn't hurt my back, I would give you a thrashing

If it were a weekend, I'd have time to sort you out once and for all

In each of these, the effect of the wording is that no assault will take place except in the stated circumstances, and the implication is that these circumstances do not exist.

immediate and unlawful violence

The threat must be of 'immediate' violence. This means if you threaten someone just as you are about to get on a train it won't be enough. You can't carry out your threat 'immediately'. The term is widely interpreted though. In **Smith v Chief Superintendent of Woking Police Station**, V was scared by D looking at her through her bedroom window at night. She was frightened of what he might do next. The CA held this was sufficient.

In **Ireland 1997**, D argued that the 'immediacy' requirement was lacking. The CA held it was satisfied because by putting himself in contact with the victims D had caused them to be in immediate fear.

Essay pointer

Is immediate fear the same thing as fear of immediate harm? The CA in **Ireland** seemed to think so. The appeal to the HL did not focus on this issue so it remains unclear. If D phones V and says, "I have planted a bomb in your house. It is set to go off in 5 minutes." there is no problem. Both the fear and the harm are immediate. However, if D says "I have planted a bomb in your house. It is set to go off in a week." then it is a different matter. V may be in immediate fear, but is not in fear of immediate harm.

On a positive note, the courts appear to be reacting to the reality of the times. In **Ireland**, the CA said, "*We must apply the law to the conditions as they are in the 20th century*".

It is now the 21st century and the law will hopefully be applied taking into account the latest methods of communication which are much more 'immediate'.

Note that in many of these cases some actual harm was also caused. This means they can come under the statutory offence of an assault occasioning actual bodily harm under **s 47 Offences Against the Persons Act 1861** as happened in **Roberts**. They are discussed here as well as in the next chapter because for **s 47** to be satisfied an assault or battery must take place first.

Essay pointer

A good argument that words should suffice is that they can sometimes be just as threatening as a gesture. As in the 'bomb' example I used earlier. Also in a society that has a sophisticated communications network the immediacy issue is more easily satisfied.

Mens rea

In **Savage1991**, Lord Ackner said, "... the mental element of assault is an intention to cause the victim to apprehend unlawful and immediate violence or recklessness whether such an apprehension is caused." That recklessness for all assaults is **Cunningham** (subjective) recklessness was confirmed in the joint appeals of **Savage & Parmenter1992**.

Applying the *mens rea* rules to assault

For **direct intent**, the prosecution must prove that it was D's aim or purpose to cause the victim to apprehend unlawful and immediate violence.

For **indirect intent**, it must be proved that it was a virtual certainty that V would apprehend immediate and unlawful violence and that D appreciated this.

For **recklessness**, it must be proved that D recognises a risk that V would apprehend immediate and unlawful violence but goes ahead and takes that risk.

Battery

Battery is the unlawful application of force to another. As noted earlier it often follows an assault. Assault and battery therefore go together in many, but not all, cases.

Example

In my earlier example of the punch on the nose, there would be both. Simon saw the punch coming, so he was in fear of harm. If Fred hit Simon from behind this would only be a battery. No assault would have occurred because Simon was not in fear.

Actus reus

The *actus reus* is the unlawful application of force to another. Both parts of the *actus reus* must be satisfied; the application of force and the fact that it is unlawful.

Application of force

It can be slight because the law sees people's bodies as inviolate. Lane LCJ said in **Faulkner and Talbot 1981**, that it was "any intentional touching of another person without the consent of that person and without lawful excuse. It need not necessarily be hostile, or rude, or aggressive, as some earlier cases seemed to indicate".

In **Thomas 1985**, the court said, "if you touch a person's clothes whilst he is wearing them that is equivalent to touching him."

In 2011, the TV presenter Fiona Bruce was sprayed with some aerosol string while she was filming an episode of Antiques Roadshow. The Ds were charged with common assault, specifically battery, for applying unlawful force.

Battery cannot be caused by an omission; there must be an act. This was confirmed in **Fagan**. D argued that not moving off the police officer's foot was an omission not an act. The court confirmed that battery could not be committed by omission, but found him guilty on the basis that there was a continuing act. The *actus reus* was the driving onto the police officer's foot and staying there.

Some early cases suggest that the force had to be direct but this is unlikely to be the case now. In **DPP v K 1990**, a schoolboy put acid in a hot air drier. Later another pupil used the drier and was badly scarred by the acid. This was held to be a battery. The case raised another issue. The boy had been using the acid in an experiment in class and was merely trying to hide it. He did not have *mens rea* when he put it in the machine, but he did have *mens rea* when he failed to do anything about it. We saw above that a battery could not be committed by omission. In **DPP v K**, omitting to rectify what he had done was held to be enough though.

In **Haystead 2000**, D punched his girlfriend who was holding her baby. She dropped the baby resulting in the baby hitting his head on the floor. The defendant was convicted of battery on the baby.

Essay pointer

Although in **Haystead** it seemed to be indirect force, it may just be a widening of the meaning of direct. The court held that direct could include *via* another person or a weapon. Thus setting a dog on someone can be seen as direct force. This is reasonable, as it is unlikely to be argued that throwing a brick at someone was not direct and there is little real difference. In civil law, apparently indirect actions have long been held to be a battery. In **Scott v Shepherd 1773**, D threw a squib into a market place. Someone picked it up and tossed it away to avoid being harmed. A second person then did the same. The third was not so quick and was injured when the squib exploded. The court held this to be a battery by D on the third person.

unlawful

In **Collins v Wilcock 1984**, a police constable who took hold of a woman's arm was acting unlawfully. If there had been a lawful arrest this would not have been the case.

Consent may make the application of force lawful. This would include things like surgery and sports. Consent may be implied. Everyday jostling and most sports contacts are not battery because there is implied consent to touching. This would not be the case if unreasonable force were used. A small nudge in the cinema queue is fine, an elbow in the ribs would not be. In a game of rugby, a tackle within the rules is fine, but a punch would not be. As both *actus reus* and *mens rea* must be proved in their entirety, there is no offence if an element is missing. Consent means the 'unlawful' element of the *actus reus* is missing. Self-defence also makes a battery lawful, but again not if unreasonable force is used.

Mens rea

As with assault, the *mens rea* is intent or recklessness. Here it is as to whether force is applied.

Task 1

Look back at the application of the rules on intent and recklessness to an assault. Apply the same rules for a case of battery.

Summary

Assault *Actus reus*	
to cause the victim to apprehend immediate and unlawful personal violence	What is the effect on the victim? Ireland
Words may be enough, or even silence	Wilson/Ireland
Mens rea	intent to cause the victim to apprehend immediate and unlawful personal violence or being subjectively reckless as to this
Battery *Actus reus*	
unlawful application of force to another	Collins v Wilcock
Can include touching V's clothes	Thomas
May include indirect force	DPP v K
Mens rea	intent to apply unlawful force or being subjectively reckless as to this

Self-test questions

What is the current definition of assault?

Can words alone constitute an assault? Use a case to support your answer.

What is the mens rea for assault?

Does a battery have to be hostile? Use a case to support your answer.

What two defences may make a battery lawful?

For some free interactive exercises visit www.drsr.org and click on Free Exercises to see what's available.

The three statutory offences are commonly called ABH, GBH and wounding but the first time you refer to these in an examination answer you need to write them in full. After that you can use the abbreviated forms.

Assault occasioning actual bodily harm (ABH) under s 47 of the Offences against the Person Act 1861

This offence comes under **s 47 Offences Against the Persons Act 1861**. It is commonly known as *ABH*. **S 47** provides:

*"whosoever shall be convicted on indictment of any **assault occasioning actual bodily harm** shall be liable to imprisonment for not more than five years"*

A clue to the *actus reus* lies in the name. The first thing that is needed is an assault, as discussed in the last chapter. This can be either an assault or a battery. In **Savage**, Lord Ackner indicated that **s 47** created two offences, an assault occasioning ABH and a battery occasioning ABH.

Therefore, this offence has the *actus reus* and *mens rea* of assault or battery plus the further *actus reus* of some harm being occasioned (i.e., caused). Let's look at this in more detail.

Actus reus

There are three parts to this.

assault – the conduct, an assault or battery

occasioning – a matter of causation

actual bodily harm – the consequence

Assault

The offence is an *assault* occasioning actual bodily harm. Assault, as we saw, covers both assault and battery. This is seen in **Savage1991**.

Key case

In **Savage**, a girl threw a glass of beer over another girl. As she did so, she let go of the glass which broke, resulting in a cut to the other girl's wrist. The throwing of the beer was enough for a battery. Lord Ackner said, *"It is of course common ground that Mrs Savage committed an assault upon Miss Beal when she threw the contents of her glass of beer over her."* In referring to assault, he is describing a battery, confirming that the word assault in **s 47** includes both assault and battery.

There was no proof she intended to throw the glass and she said it was an accident. However, she did intend to throw the beer. The throwing of the beer was enough for the *actus reus* of battery. She intended to do this, so there was *mens rea* too. Once battery was proved, for her to be convicted under **s 47** the prosecution merely had to show this had 'occasioned' (caused) the harm.

So, 'assault' for **s 47** requires the *actus reus* and *mens rea* of an assault or a battery. Now to 'occasioning'.

occasioning

Occasioning means bringing about, or causing. **S 47** is a result crime so the prosecution must show that the assault or battery caused the result (actual bodily harm). D's actions must make a significant contribution to the harm and the chain of causation must not be broken.

Task 2

Look back at Chapter 1 on *actus reus* and causation. Read **Roberts** to remind yourself of the facts. The question was whether the battery by D caused the harm. Why did the action by the victim not break the chain of causation? What type of action might do so?

In **Savage**, the HL said that once the assault was established, the only remaining question was whether the victim's conduct was the natural consequence of that assault. According to Lord Ackner,

> *"the word 'occasioning' raised solely a question of causation, an objective question which does not involve inquiring into the accused's state of mind".*

Occasioning therefore relates to *actus reus* not *mens rea*. There is no need to intend any harm at all.

Examination tip

Causation is a common issue in a problem question where a result crime like ABH is involved. If harm has occurred, you may need to discuss all three of these offences. You will certainly have to discuss two of them because **s 47** cannot happen without one of the others. You will need to define and explain assault and/or battery. Then define harm. Finally show that the assault (or battery) caused the harm. Use a case like **Roberts** or **Savage** to explain this and apply it to the facts given. If those facts remind you of a more relevant case, use that instead.

Finally, you will need to explain *mens rea*, but only as regards the assault. We'll come back to this.

actual bodily harm

In **Miller 1954**, this was held to be any hurt or injury calculated to 'interfere with health or comfort', which could include mental discomfort. In **Chan-Fook 1994**, the CA qualified this a little. Psychiatric injury was enough but not "mere emotions" such as fear, distress or panic, and really trivial or insignificant harm is excluded. Some type of identifiable medical condition will be needed, but it is clear that harm is not confined to physical injury.

In **DPP v Ross Smith 2006**, the QBD held that cutting someone's hair without consent amounted to assault occasioning actual bodily harm. At trial, the magistrate had accepted that as the victim had suffered no physical or psychological harm the offence was not proved. The QBD disagreed. Referring to **Chan-Fook** and **Burstow**, it was held that 'harm' included hurt or damage and 'actual' meant merely that it was not trivial harm. 'Bodily' harm applied to all parts of the body, of which hair was a part, and her hair had been cut so there was 'bodily harm'. The court also held that pain was not a necessary requirement of actual bodily harm.

Key case

In **Ireland 1996**, silent 'phone calls which caused psychiatric harm came under **s 47**. D's argument was that there was no assault because there was no fear of 'immediate' harm. If there was no assault, there could be no assault occasioning actual bodily harm. The argument failed as the court found sufficient 'immediacy' in a telephone call. Swinton LJ, in the CA, said that:

> *"It has been recognised for many centuries that putting a person in fear may amount to an assault. The early cases predate the invention of the telephone. We must apply the law to the conditions as they are in the 20th century".*

This comment was approved in the HL.

The CA also relied on **Chan-Fook** to confirm that psychiatric harm was enough for 'bodily harm'.

Mens rea

The *mens rea* of assault is intent or recklessness to cause assault or unlawful force (**Venna 1976**).

D need not intend, or be reckless as to, any harm, only the assault or battery. This was held to be the case by the CA in **Roberts 1971**. D argued that he did not intend to cause harm and nor was he reckless. He was found guilty because he had the *mens rea* and the *actus reus* for the battery, plus harm had been caused. This was enough for **s 47**. Despite this seemingly clear principle of law, there was conflict in several cases over the next 20 years.

Key case

The issue was finally put beyond doubt by the HL in the joint appeals of **Savage & Parmenter 1992**. These two cases had been decided differently in the lower courts. The principle of **Roberts** had been followed in **Savage** but not in **Parmenter**.

In **Savage & Parmenter**, the HL held **Roberts** to be the correct law. The throwing of the beer with intent to do so was enough for a battery. The question for the court was whether a further mental state had to be established in relation to the bodily harm element of the **s 47** offence. Lord Ackner said, *"Clearly the section, by its terms, expressly imposes no such requirement"*.

This means that if D has *mens rea* for the assault and additionally harm occurs, it can amount to the more serious charge under **s 47**. Think about it as an equation:

Assault (AR + MR of assault or battery) + occasions (AR, causation) + harm (AR consequence) = **s 47**

Example

Sandra shouts threateningly at Tara. Tara is scared that Sandra will hit her. She jumps back and hits her head causing severe bruising. This will be enough for a charge under **s 47**. There is the *actus reus* of an assault (Tara is in fear of immediate violence) plus *mens rea* (Sandra intends to frighten her) and this assault occasioned (caused – jumping back and falling is foreseeable, as in **Roberts**) actual bodily harm (severe bruising).

So, the *mens rea* for **s 47** is intent or subjective recklessness as to the assault only, not the harm. The prosecution will have to show one of the following:

> **Direct intent:** causing fear of violence or the application of force is D's aim or purpose.

> **Indirect intent:** D appreciates that it is virtually certain that the V will fear violence, or D appreciates that the application of force is virtually certain.

> **Subjective recklessness:** D is aware of the risk of V being in fear, or is aware of the risk of force being applied, and goes ahead anyway.

Essay pointer

One problem with **s 47** is that the *mens rea* does not match the *actus reus*. For the *actus reus* of **s 47** you need ABH to have occurred, the *mens rea* is only for assault or battery though (**Roberts**, **Savage**). This is confusing, and arguably unfair. Should D be guilty of causing ABH where there was only intent to scare someone? On the other hand, should D get away with harming someone when the attempt to scare them caused harm?

Task 3 Case study

In **DPP v Smith (Michael) 2006**, D held down his ex-girlfriend and cut off her ponytail with a pair of kitchen scissors. In the Magistrates court he was acquitted because, although there was an assault (specifically a battery), it was held that it had not caused any actual bodily harm. There was no injury such as bruising or bleeding, and no evidence of psychiatric harm. The magistrates held that her distress was not sufficient for actual bodily harm. On appeal, the QBD rejected D's argument that hair was only dead tissue and so did not amount to bodily harm. Judge P said:

> "Even if, medically and scientifically speaking, the hair above the surface of the scalp is no more than dead tissue, it remains part of the body and is attached to it. While it is so attached, in my judgment it falls within the meaning of 'bodily' in the phrase 'actual bodily harm'. It is concerned with the body of the individual victim".

Cresswell J agreed and said:

> "Where a significant portion of a woman's hair is cut off without her consent, this is a serious matter amounting to actual (not trivial or insignificant) bodily harm".

What was Smith charged with at the Magistrates' court?

Which other charge might have been more successful? Give reasons and/or cases in support.

What was the main reason that Judge P gave for finding the cutting of hair to be 'bodily' harm?

Which case decided that ABH was any hurt or injury calculated to 'interfere with health or comfort'?

Cresswell J said it was serious and not 'trivial or insignificant'. Which case decided that trivial harm was not ABH?

The magistrates held that her distress was not sufficient for actual bodily harm. Which case do you think they followed?

Do you think the magistrates or the QBD were right?

Summary of s 47

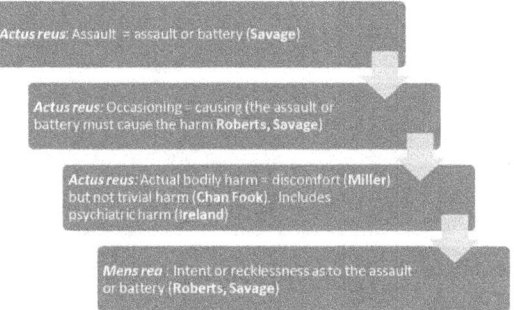

Actus reus: Assault = assault or battery (**Savage**)

Actus reus: Occasioning = causing (the assault or battery must cause the harm **Roberts, Savage**)

Actus reus: Actual bodily harm = discomfort (**Miller**) but not trivial harm (**Chan Fook**). Includes psychiatric harm (**Ireland**)

Mens rea : Intent or recklessness as to the assault or battery (**Roberts, Savage**)

17

Self-test questions

Who said, "We must apply the law to the conditions as they are in the 20th century" and in which case?

What are the three parts to the actus reus of ABH?

For which part of the actus reus is mens rea needed?

Which case was relied on in **Ireland** to support the point that ABH includes psychiatric harm?

In which case did the HL finally confirm that the principle in **Roberts** was correct?

Grievous bodily harm (GBH) and wounding under s 20 and s 18 of the Offences against the Person Act 1861

"In the context of a criminal act therefore the words 'cause' and 'inflict' may be taken to be interchangeable"

Lord Hope

Section 20 makes it an offence to:

> *"**unlawfully and maliciously wound or inflict any grievous bodily harm** upon any other person, either with or without any weapon or instrument"*

Section 18 makes it an offence to:

> *"unlawfully and maliciously by any means whatsoever wound or cause any grievous bodily harm to any person with intent to do some grievous bodily harm to any person"*

These two offences are commonly called malicious wounding (**s 20**) and wounding with intent (**s 18**). However, there are actually two separate offences under each section.

> **unlawfully and maliciously wounding**

> **unlawfully and maliciously inflicting / causing grievous bodily harm**

There is very little difference in the *actus reus*; each needs **either** a wound **or** serious injury. We will deal with the two sections together for *actus reus* and then look at the different *mens rea* for each.

Actus reus for s 18 and s 20

There are four matters to consider.

> **unlawfully**

> **wound**

> **inflict / cause**

> **grievous bodily harm**

We'll take these in turn. I have left out 'malicious' for the moment as this has been treated as relating to *mens rea*.

unlawfully

If the act is done lawfully, no offence has occurred. Thus if D has acted in self-defence this makes it lawful, so part of the *actus reus* is missing. Consent may also make it lawful.

In **Clarence 1888**, D, knowing he had a sexually transmitted disease, had sex with his wife. She caught the disease. This amounted to grievous bodily harm. D's conviction was quashed on the basis that the sex was by consent and it made no difference that the wife did not know about the disease.

This is more limited now. In **Brown 1994**, the House of Lords decided that consent of the victim could no longer be a defence if serious harm was *intended*. In **Dica 2004**, D had consensual sex with two women knowing he was HIV positive. They both became infected with HIV and he was convicted under **s 20** with recklessly inflicting grievous bodily harm. On appeal, the CA confirmed the point in **Brown** that consent was not a defence to *intentional* harm. However, as the charge was *recklessly* inflicting grievous bodily harm, they held that the issue of consent should not have been withdrawn from the jury. A retrial was ordered.

wound

Key case

In **C v Eisenhower 1983**, a wound was defined as being 'any puncture of the skin'. The case involved a child firing an air gun. The pellet hit V in the eye but did not break the skin. It was held that internal bleeding caused by the rupture of an internal organ was not a wound. Therefore, something that does not break the skin, such as an abrasion, bruise or burn would not amount to a wound.

inflict and cause – is there a difference?

The *actus reus* of **s 20** is to unlawfully and maliciously wound or *'inflict'* grievous bodily harm. The *actus reus* of **s 18** is to unlawfully and maliciously wound or *'cause'* grievous bodily harm. In **Clarence**, the word 'inflict' was held to mean that a prior assault was required, as for **s 47**. Other cases seem to have ignored this requirement. In **Wilson 1984**, the HL held that a person could be charged under **s 20** without an assault. They relied on the Australian case of **Salisbury 1976** where it was said that 'inflict' does not imply assault is needed. However it was said that the word 'inflict' did mean that *direct* application of force was needed. It was therefore narrower than the word 'cause'.

Essay pointer

This uncertainty has been clarified. Both **Salisbury** and **Wilson** were approved by the HL in **Ireland & Burstow**. In the CA Lord Bingham had said it would be *"an affront to common sense"* to distinguish between the two offences in this way. The HL confirmed that liability for GBH could occur without the application of direct or indirect force, and rejected the argument that 'inflict' was narrower than 'cause'. Lord Hope made the statement in the opening quote. **Clarence** was referred to as a "troublesome authority". In **Dica**, the CA again confirmed that there was no requirement of assault for a charge under **s 20**.

A factor worth noting (as it was by the HL in **Ireland & Burstow**) is that the **1861 Act** consolidated several different Acts. Therefore, the difference in the two sections is not as significant as it would be had they been written at the same time.

One criticism is that if there is no requirement of assault in **s 20** then it is hard to justify convicting D of *assault* occasioning actual bodily harm as an alternative, as was confirmed again in **Savage and Parmenter**.

Grievous bodily harm

This is commonly called GBH. In **Smith 1961**, grievous was interpreted by the HL to mean 'really serious'. In **Saunders 1985**, the CA held that the word 'really' was unnecessary. Thus, GBH includes *any* serious harm. In **Burstow 1996**, a campaign of harassment by D, which led to V suffering severe depressive illness, was charged under **s 20**. In the joint appeals to the HL in **Ireland & Burstow 1997**, the HL confirmed that psychiatric harm could come under **s 47**, **s 18** or **s 20**.

Serious harm is usually required, but note should be taken of **Bollom 2004**. A baby suffered bruising to several parts of her body and her mother's partner was charged with GBH. Although the CA substituted the conviction for one of ABH, it was made clear that bruising could amount to GBH if the victim was a young child. This means the age of the victim may be relevant in deciding the appropriate charge. Presumably, this argument could also be applied to an old or vulnerable person.

A wound may occur without GBH. Conversely, GBH may occur without a wound.

Example

Let's reconsider two cases we saw when looking at **s 47**.

In **Savage**, the glass broke and cut the other girl. This is technically a wound as the skin has been broken. She could have been charged with wounding under **s 20**. It would not be 'serious' harm though, so no charge of inflicting GBH would succeed.

In the joint appeals of **Ireland & Burstow**, the HL said psychiatric harm could amount to GBH. This type of harm could not be a wound though.

Examination tip

Look for clues in the scenario. If it refers to a cut then discuss wounding under either **s 18** or **s 20**. If it is only a small cut you could discuss **s 47**. If a serious internal injury is mentioned then discuss GBH. In all cases, the prosecution must establish a chain of causation. D's act must make a *significant contribution* to the wound or harm (see Chapter 1).

S 20 refers to 'with or without any weapon or instrument'. **S 18** refers to 'by any means whatsoever'. Remember these offences came from different Acts and were not written at the same time. It doesn't matter *how* D inflicts or causes the harm. However, the use of a weapon may help in establishing intent to cause serious harm, and so point you at **s 18**.

Mens rea

It is important to be able to identify the different *mens rea* in **s 18** and **s 20**. There are two differences: the type of *mens rea* and the type of harm that the *mens rea* relates to.

Both sections contain the word 'maliciously'. This does not mean spite or ill will, as we might view the word. As regards **s 20**, the CA interpreted it in **Cunningham 1957** as meaning intent or subjective recklessness (see Chapter 1). For **s 18**, it would appear that the word maliciously is unnecessary. In **Mowatt**, the judge said, "*In s 18 the word 'maliciously' adds nothing*".

Mens rea for s 20

As noted above this is intent or subjective recklessness. However, D need not intend or recognise the risk of serious harm. Intending or seeing the risk (*mens rea*) of *some* harm is enough as long as the result (*actus reus*) is serious harm. This was confirmed by the CA in **Mowatt 1968** and later approved by the HL in **Savage & Parmenter 1992**.

Key case

In **Parmenter** D threw his baby into the air and caused GBH when he caught it. His argument that he lacked *mens rea* succeeded. He had not seen the risk of *any* injury (he'd done it before several times with older children) so he was not guilty.

It is only necessary to prove that D foresaw some harm *might* occur. It is not necessary to prove that D foresaw that some harm *would* occur. This point was confirmed in **DPP v A 2000**. Here a 13-year-old boy shot his friend whilst they were playing with two air pistols. His argument that he lacked *mens rea* was rejected. The case is similar to **Eisenhower**.

In **Jones v First-Tier Tribunal 2011**, the CA held that for a charge of GBH there was no need to prove that the action was hostile. D had run in front of a lorry and the driver was injured. D argued he had no *mens rea* as he had only intended to harm himself, not anyone else and the tribunal had accepted this argument. The CA held, however, that it was foreseeable that harm could be caused to the driver of the lorry; therefore, the *mens rea* of recklessness could be proved for the **s 20** offence. In **Jones v FTT 2013**, the SC allowed D's appeal. The SC noted that the CA had decided that anyone running into a busy road must have at least seen the risk of some harm and, referring to **Parmenter,** held this was sufficient *mens rea* for **s 20**. However, the SC said that the question of whether D *himself* foresaw harm was a matter for the tribunal and not an appeal court, and reinstated the tribunal's decision.

Essay pointer

S 18 and **s 20** involve *either* GBH *or* wounding. The first has been interpreted as 'really serious' harm (**Smith**), however wounding has been interpreted as an 'open cut' (**Eisenhower**), which could be quite trivial. The prosecution failed to prove D had inflicted a wound in **Eisenhower** because there was no open cut and thus no 'wound'. This case highlights the need to get the charge right. A charge of GBH could have succeeded. Another issue is that, as for **s 47**, the *mens rea* does not match the *actus reus*. For **s 20**, you need serious harm to have occurred, but the *mens rea* is only for some harm (**Mowatt**).

Application of *mens rea* for s 20

> **Direct intent: It is D's aim to cause *some harm*.**

> **Indirect intent: *Some harm* is a virtual certainty and D appreciates this.**

> **Subjective recklessness: D recognises the risk of *some harm* and goes ahead anyway.**

Mens rea for s 18

The *mens rea* for **s 18** is specific intent, i.e., intent only. It was confirmed in **Belfon**, where D had slashed someone with a razor, that recklessness was not enough, there must be intent to cause serious harm. **S 18** says *"with intent to do some grievous bodily harm"*. It was confirmed in **Parmenter** that for **s 18** D must intend *serious harm*. This is the vital difference and makes **s 18** much more serious, leading to a possible maximum life sentence. **S 20** carries a maximum of 5 years.

A further difference with **s 18** *mens rea* is that it includes intent to resist or prevent a lawful arrest. The problem with this is that it is added as an alternative to intent to cause GBH, so has been interpreted as meaning that if the situation is resisting or preventing an arrest, intent is only needed for that, not the harm. This is seen in **Morrison 1989** where D dived through a window resisting arrest and a police officer was badly cut. The CA upheld his conviction and held that it was enough that he intended resisting arrest. Regarding GBH, the word 'malicious' suggested that intent OR recklessness was enough, and he had been reckless.

Essay pointer

If **s 18** requires serious harm in both *actus reus* and *mens rea*, then arguably so should **s 20**. There is still a difference in the *mens rea* because **s 18** requires intent to be proved.

Another issue is sentencing. The maximum sentences for **s 20** and **s 18** are very different. The maximum for **s 20** is the same as **s 47**, i.e., 5 years. This seems strange. Life for **s 18** can be justified in that intent seriously to injure is also the *mens rea* for murder. Which charge is brought will depend on the chance factor of whether the victim dies or not. The same sentence for **s 47** and **s 20** is harder to justify. In **Parmenter**, the CA. noted there was an overlap between **s 47** and **s 20** but indicated that **s 20** was a more serious offence. The Law Commission proposes a maximum of 5 years for **s 47**, as now, but a maximum 7 years for **s 20**. This seems more realistic – but the reforms may be a long way off becoming reality.

A further recommendation by the Law Commission is that **s 18** would be 'intentional serious injury' and **s 20** would be 'reckless serious injury'. This would clear up the problem of the *mens rea*. It is arguably unfair to charge someone with GBH when the *mens rea* was only for some harm. A final criticism of the current law is that there are two different offences in each section. This makes four offences in all, which is unnecessarily complicated

The Law Commission is starting a new project in 2014.

The Commission notes that the Act is widely recognised as being outdated and that it uses archaic language. It also says that the structure of the Act is unsatisfactory; because there is no clear hierarchy of offences and the differences between **sections 18, 20** and **47** are not clearly spelt out.

The following is a quote from their site in 2012.

> *"Section 20 (maliciously wounding or inflicting grievous bodily harm) is seen as more serious than section 47 (assault occasioning actual bodily harm) but the maximum penalty (five years) is the same. Furthermore the actus reus for sections 18 (intentionally wounding or causing grievous bodily harm) and 20 appear to be the same apart from the distinction between "causing" and "inflicting", which is notoriously difficult to draw.*
>
> *This project will therefore aim to restructure the law on offences against the person, probably by creating a structured hierarchy of offences, as well as modernising and simplifying the language by which these offences are defined".*

Application of *mens rea* for s 18

   Direct intent: It is D's aim or purpose to cause *grievous bodily harm*

   Indirect intent: *Grievous bodily harm* is a virtual certainty and D appreciates this

Which charge?

It was confirmed in **Savage** that a jury could bring in **s 20** as an alternative verdict when someone is charged under **s 18** and **s 47** as an alternative to **s 20**. If not, the conviction may be changed on appeal. In **Bollom 2004**, the conviction for GBH under **s 20** was reduced by the CA to ABH under **s 47**. Alternatively, D may put in a plea before or during the trial.

Example

In **Topp 2011**, (unreported) a woman bit her boyfriend's testicles. He needed several stitches and she was charged with wounding with intent under **s 18**. Prior to the trial, she pleaded guilty to **s 20**, arguing she did not intend serious harm. The prosecution accepted the alternative plea.

Sometimes both charges are brought so the prosecution can be more confident of getting a conviction – and to avoid the error of bringing the wrong charge as in **Eisenhower**.

Example

In **Hargreaves 2010**, D was in a taxi with her boyfriend and another man, all of whom had been drinking. She was in the back and was having an argument with her boyfriend, who was sitting in the front. He turned towards her and she kicked out at him, ramming a stiletto heel through his eye and into his brain. She was charged with both grievous bodily harm with intent under **s 18**, and an alternative charge of inflicting grievous bodily harm under **s 20**.

On the facts, she was acquitted because she had kicked out at him believing he was going to attack her and so successfully pleaded self-defence.

Examination tip

All this means you may need to discuss all three statutory offences. Explain the *actus reus* of either GBH or wounding as appropriate, using cases in support. Note carefully the difference in the *mens rea* as this may help you to decide which section is most appropriate. Thus if you go for **s 18**, explain and apply the law (with cases) but then say that if the prosecution can't prove intent to cause GBH then D may be convicted of **s 20** instead. If you go for **s 20**, you can then discuss **s 47** if you feel the harm may not be serious enough.

Summary

Actus reus	
Inflict or cause	Mean the same thing (Ireland)
Wound	Open cut (Eisenhower)
Grievous bodily harm	Serious harm (Smith/Saunders)
Mens rea	
S 20 Intent or recklessness	To cause some harm (Mowatt)
S 18 Intent only	To cause serious harm (Parmenter)

Self-test questions

How has 'wound' been interpreted?

How has 'grievous bodily harm' been interpreted?

Which cases can you use to support your answers to the above questions?

*What is the difference in the mens rea between **s 20** and **s 18**?*

*What are the maximum sentences for **s 20** and **s 18** respectively?*

For some free interactive exercises visit www.drsr.org and click on Free Exercises to see what's available.

Revision

A general guide to revision

The first and foremost rule for revision is to start early. Too many students leave it until the last minute and then get in a panic. If you take it gently and organise your time properly you will feel a lot more calm and confident when exam time comes. Make a plan of what you want to cover each day and try to stick to it. Don't forget to include some breaks in your schedule, if you are tired it will be harder to retain the material you have been revising.

Here are a few tips for revision techniques

Go through your notes and try to summarise them

Learn the key cases, as these are essential to know

Make sure you understand how the judge has applied the law to the facts so you can do the same in an examination scenario

If the case is one you may also want to use in an essay, be sure you understand any problems it raises or solves and / or the concept of law that is involved

Example

In **Brown**, the judges decided that consent was not a defence to serious harm, so this would apply to a scenario involving GBH.

It raises a problem in the law, because the reasoning was obscure. It was not sufficiently clear why the consent defence failed. It could be argued that the defence fails if harm was intended (this would apply to s 18 but not 20), or alternatively that the defence fails if harm was serious (this would apply to both s 18 and 20).

Another problem, and one which relates to the concept of law and morals, is that some of the judges seemed to rely on their own moral values when reaching their decision.

Go through the summaries of the topic, these provide a base of the essential points which may need to be addressed

Go to the examination board's website for past exam papers, mark schemes and reports

Practice answering questions then look at the examiners' mark schemes and reports to see if you were on the right track

Revision of the non-fatal offences

The main thing with these five offences is to be able to distinguish between them. Here is a summary of all the offences with a brief explanation of what is required in each case.

Offence	Actus Reus	Mens Rea	Case example	Type of harm
Assault	to cause the victim to apprehend immediate and unlawful personal harm	intent or subjective recklessness to cause fear of harm	AR: Ireland/Smith v Woking) MR: Savage	None, just fear of it

25

	violence			
Battery	unlawful application of force to another	intent or subjective recklessness to apply force	AR: Collins v Wilcock/Thomas MR: Venna	None, any application of force will do – even touching clothing (Thomas)
Assault occasioning actual bodily harm – s 47 OAPA 1861	An assault (assault or battery) which causes harm	intent or subjective recklessness for the assault or battery only	AR: Chan Fook MR: Savage/ Roberts	Any small injury such as bruises, sprains, small cuts or psychiatric harm etc. (but note very minor injuries are usually treated as battery rather than ABH)
Malicious Wounding – s 20 OAPA 1861	unlawful and malicious wounding or inflicting grievous (serious) bodily harm	intent or subjective recklessness to inflict some harm	AR: Wound - C v Eisenhower AR: GBH – Saunders MR: Mowatt	A wound or serious injury such as broken bones, internal injuries etc.
Wounding with intent – s 18 OAPA 1861	unlawful and malicious wounding or causing grievous (serious) bodily harm	intent (only) to cause serious harm	AR: Wound - C v Eisenhower AR: GBH – Saunders MR: Parmenter	A wound or serious injury such as broken bones, internal injuries etc.

Examples

Dan followed Liz home from work every evening and she became so frightened that she suffered severe anxiety. This would be an assault as Dan has caused fear, and assault can be by words or even silence (**Ireland/Smith v Woking**). Stalking was held to amount to an assault in **Constanza,** and this is similar. Liz has suffered 'severe anxiety' and this would amount to ABH (**Chan-Fook/Ireland**). There is no need for Dan to intend or be reckless as to the harm (**Roberts/Savage**), as long as he saw the risk of causing fear he will have **Cunningham** recklessness for the assault and this is enough. As the anxiety is 'severe', it could amount to GBH (**Burstow**). It was confirmed in **Savage** that a jury could bring in **s 47** as an alternative verdict when someone is charged under to **s 20**, so the charge could be **s 20** GBH and if the harm is not seen as sufficiently serious the conviction would be for **s 47**. The other problem with a charge under **s 20** is that it would have to be shown that Dan was at least reckless as to causing some harm and this may be difficult as there is no evidence he foresaw the risk of harming Liz, he was only following her.

Andy ran up to Steve waving a stick and shouting. As Steve ran away, Andy threw the stick at him and Steve fell over grazing his knee. This is assault because Steve was obviously in fear of violence as he ran away. It is also a battery as Andy threw the stick at him, and battery can be indirect (**DPP v K/Haystead**). Running away from a threat is foreseeable so does not break the chain of causation between the assault and the grazed knee (**Roberts**). This means a charge of ABH is also possible, although the injury is minor so it may only be battery, it was said in **Chan-Fook** that trivial harm would not amount to ABH.

Several rules have been established by case law over the years.

Task 4

Make a note of the cases which established the following *actus reus* rules

Assault can be by silence
Words may negate an assault
Immediate is interpreted widely
Battery can be indirect
Battery can include touching someone's clothing
Everyday social contact (e.g., jostling in a queue, a tap on the shoulder) will not amount to a battery because there is implied consent to such actions
ABH can include psychiatric harm as long as this is more than mere emotions
ABH can include cutting someone's hair without consent
Occasioning is a matter of causation so if D causes the harm that is enough even if neither intended nor done recklessly
GBH can include psychiatric harm if it is serious
GBH can include less serious harm in the case of a child
GBH can include the transmission of disease if intentional
A wound requires both layers of the skin to be cut
S 18 includes intent to resist or prevent a lawful arrest and where this is the case the MR as regards the harm is lower. It is enough that D is reckless

Task 5

What is the minimum *mens rea* for the three statutory offences? Apply the rules on *mens rea* to each of these offences

Key criticisms

We have seen many problems whilst looking at the individual offences and it is in clear the **Offences Against the Person Act 1861** is in need of reform. There are also more general issues:

Language: the **Act** is very complicated and was written in 1861, so much of the language is obscure. Lawyers and juries have struggled to understand the complexities of the different offences. The courts also have difficulty interpreting words such as 'occasioning', 'actual bodily harm', 'grievous' and 'maliciously' as they are not used in the same sense today. This can result in conflicting case law and injustice. The word 'maliciously' has been interpreted as meaning recklessly (**Parmenter**). However it appears in **s 18** as well as **s 20** and the *mens rea* for **s 18** is intent only. In **Parmenter,** the judge had difficulty explaining 'maliciously' to the jury. He said that it meant that it was enough that D *should have foreseen* that some harm might occur. This sounds very like objective rather than subjective recklessness. In fact, on appeal, this was said to be a misdirection. It highlights the fact that these words need to be clearly explained.

Common law: assault and battery are outside the **Act**. Clarity would require all the offences to be together in one place. However, an alternative argument is that the common law can keep them up to date. This happened in **Ireland,** where it was recognised that an assault could be *via* a telephone.

Proposals for reform have been produced and Bills put before Parliament over a long period of time, but to date Parliament has not found time to debate the issues – see below under proposed reforms

Proposed reforms

The Law Commission has been considering codification of the criminal law for some time. This was a huge task and so it was decided it would be better to work on a series of self-contained bills to deal with different parts of the criminal law. In 1993 the Commission produced a report (**No 218**) and draft Bill on the non-fatal offences against the person. This never received parliamentary time but in 1998 the government produced its own Bill incorporating most of the recommended changes, but again little happened. The Commission is now readdressing the issue. They note on their site (have a look under 'On-going projects' in criminal law) that the Act is outdated and uses archaic language. They particularly refer to the lack of a clear hierarchy, noting **s 20** is seen as more serious than **s 47** but has the same maximum sentence; and to the problem caused by the different words of 'cause' and 'inflict' in **s 18** and **s 20**. The intention is to restructure the law and modernise and simplify the language.

No Bill has yet received parliamentary time, something that can be added to the other criticisms of the law. The table below shows the proposals from the 1998 Bill. The offences are redefined and in all of them the *mens rea* matches the *actus reus*. The Law Commission project started in 2014 is likely to result in something very similar, although we cannot be sure at this stage.

Name of proposed offence	Explanation of proposed offence	Current offence
Intentional serious injury	Clause 1: intentionally causing serious injury	**S 18**
Reckless serious injury	Clause 2: recklessly causing serious injury	**S 20**
Intentional or reckless injury	Clause 3: intentionally or recklessly causing injury	**S 47**
Assault	Clause 4: intentionally or recklessly applying force to or causing an impact on the body of another; or intentionally or recklessly causing	Common assault (assault and battery)

another to believe force is imminent

In each case the word 'cause' is used. The Bill also defines injury to include both physical and psychiatric harm. It excludes any harm caused by disease except for Clause 1. This is in line with **Dica.**

Task 6

Look back at the essay pointers and key criticisms. Write some notes on these with case examples, and add your own thoughts. Then read the proposed reforms. Ask yourself whether these reforms would solve any of the problems you have identified, and add this to your notes.

Keep these notes for revision and as a guide to evaluation questions.

For some free interactive exercises visit www.drsr.org and click on Free Exercises to see what's available.

Although different exam boards have different ways of styling their examination papers, there are always going to be common elements. You will need to be able to apply the law you have learnt to a particular scenario, and you will need to be able to evaluate a given topic to provide a critique of the law, including reforms where appropriate.

A general guide to examination papers

Read **all** questions carefully before deciding which to answer

Look again at the ones you wish to answer to make sure you can do so, make brief notes - this can be a useful checklist later when you are tired and your memory begins to fail.

Structure your answer. Remember this is a test of law so you need to state the legal principles involved and apply them to the particular question. A solid start is worth a lot and gets the examiner on your side. A small plan is helpful.

It is necessary to do more than regurgitate your notes. You need to be selective as to what is relevant, and to choose appropriate cases and examples in support of what you say.

Never put in irrelevant material just because you know it - there is **never** a question asking you to 'write all you know about...'. The examiner wants to know that you understand the specific issues and can apply the appropriate law to the facts given.

Always support your answer with **relevant** cases. Don't worry too much about the facts, the principle forming the *ratio decidendi* is usually the important part e.g. in **Donoghue v Stevenson** that you owe a duty to others to take care is vital but you don't need to write a paragraph discussing snails and ginger beer.

Having said that, you want to show why you have chosen a particular case so will need to mention any facts that specifically relate to the scenario. If the scenario mentions someone being ill after consuming a chocolate bar with a dead mouse in it (yes, there has been a case!) then talking briefly about snails in ginger beer will be relevant. The main point here is that you need to be selective; this demonstrates a skill in itself and conserves precious time.

If you can't remember the name of a case that is relevant, don't leave it out but refer to it in a general way e.g. 'in one decided case....' or 'in a similar case....'

In problem questions, identify the various issues in the first paragraph and then set about dealing with them one by one, applying the relevant law and cases to each issue, **referring to the facts of the question as you do so**. This tells the examiner that you are answering the specific points raised. A short summing up is also a good idea e.g., "In conclusion it would appear that D may be liable for ... but it is possible that the defence of ... applies which will reduce/negate liability".

In essay questions, you will usually be asked to form an opinion or to weigh up arguments for and against a particular statement. Here a broader range of knowledge is needed showing arguments for, arguments against and an evaluation of these arguments. If reforms have been proposed or implemented, discuss these too. You should always round off your answer with a short concluding paragraph, preferably using some of the wording from the question to indicate to the examiner that you are addressing the specific issue raised.

Essays should have a logical structure. The beginning, should introduce the subject matter, the central part should explain/analyse/criticise it as appropriate, and the conclusion should bring the various strands of argument together with reference to the question set.

Try to consider alternative arguments. A well-rounded essay will bring in other views even if you disagree with them; you cannot shoot them down without setting them up first.

Essay writing is a skill in itself, so here is a brief guide on how to structure your essay.

Writing a discussion essay: staging the information logically

If you stage your essay as follows, it will make it easy to read, logically structured and easier to write. It may also mean you don't leave out important points. Here's how it works:

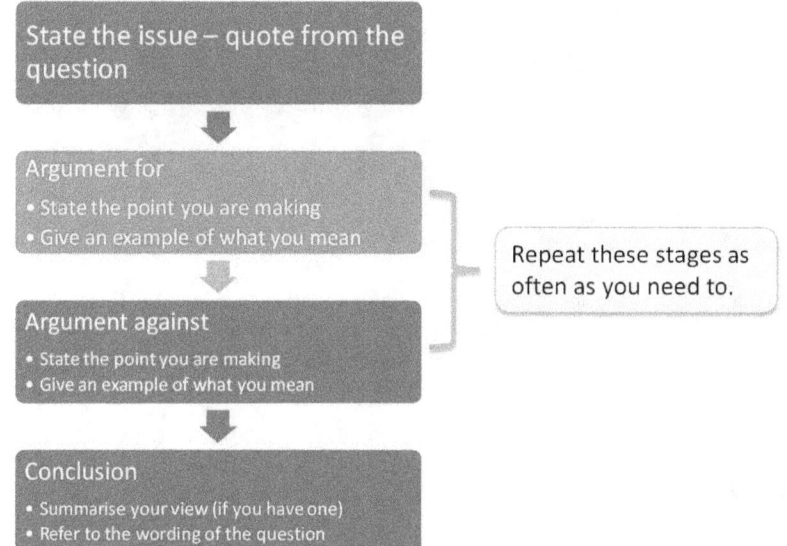

State the issue – quote from the question

Argument for
• State the point you are making
• Give an example of what you mean

Argument against
• State the point you are making
• Give an example of what you mean

Repeat these stages as often as you need to.

Conclusion
• Summarise your view (if you have one)
• Refer to the wording of the question

Writing each paragraph: making each one logical and easy to read (and write!)

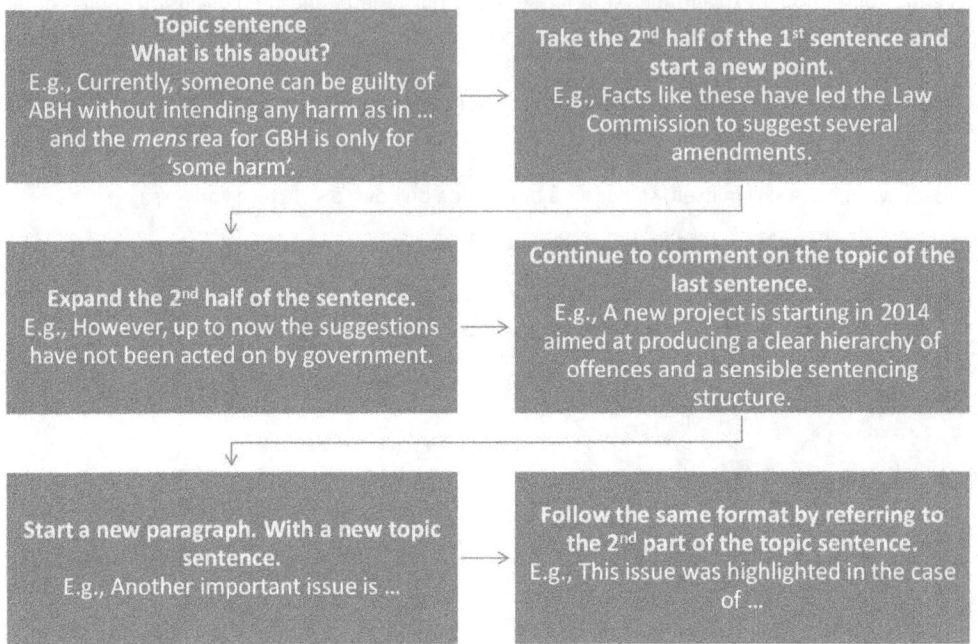

Finally, make sure you cover the whole question. For both problem and evaluation questions, there are only a certain number of marks available. The examiner has a mark scheme to work to, so however brilliant your answer to one part of the question is, missing out the other parts will severely reduce your total marks.

Examination practice for non-fatal offences

Problem scenarios (application)

The law on *actus reus* and *mens rea* prepares you for answering problem questions on this topic, e.g., we saw that battery cannot be committed by an omission; it requires an act (**Fagan**). Of particular importance with these offences is causation and *mens rea*.

Most of the offences are result crimes so it must be proved that D's act caused the result actually (**White**) and in law (**Cheshire**). The result in each case changes with the offence. Assault requires that V is in fear of violence, ABH requires some harm or injury, GBH and wounding require serious harm or a cut.

Assault, battery, ABH and GBH/wounding under **s 20** all require the *mens rea* of intent (**Nedrick/Woollin**) or subjective recklessness (**Cunningham**). These vary with the offences and note in particular ABH under **s 47** and GBH under **s 20** where the *mens rea* does not match the *actus reus*. The first requires *mens rea* only for an assault or battery and the latter requires *mens rea* only for *some* harm, not *serious* harm.

S 18 requires the *mens rea* of intent to cause *serious* harm; recklessness is not enough, nor is intent to cause *some* harm.

Examination tip

Application of the law requires you to be selective. The facts should point you to particular issues which need addressing and you must be prepared to pick out the relevant law and cases and to leave out anything irrelevant – for which you will gain no marks.

Examples

Franz is having an argument with Sergei. He pulls out a knife and stabs Sergei in the arm. Sergei is taken to hospital where he has to have several stitches.

Here there is no need to discuss assault, battery or ABH. The words 'several stitches' show the harm is serious enough for GBH and that there is also a wound. The two offences you should discuss are GBH and/or wounding under **s 20** and **s 18.** A charge under either section is possible as the *actus reus* is the same. Explain harm must be serious (**Saunders**), and several stitches indicates that it is, and that a cut needing stitches will be a wound as described in **Eisenhower**, because both layers of the skin must have been cut to need stitches. Then discuss the rules on *mens rea*. This is what will decide the charge. As Franz 'pulled out a knife', it would indicate that he had sufficient *mens rea* for **s 18**. This requires that he intended serious harm. Even if serious harm was not his aim or purpose, which is how direct intent was described in **Mohan**, the jury are likely to decide that he appreciated that serious harm was a virtual certainty as a result of stabbing Sergei, so he will have indirect intent as established in **Nedrick** and confirmed in **Woollin**. If the jury were not convinced that he intended serious harm, then the alternative charge under **s 20** would be easy to prove. **Mowatt** confirms that *mens rea* is only needed for some harm, not serious harm. Franz would have at least foreseen the risk of some harm resulting, and this is **Cunningham** recklessness, which is enough for **s 20**.

Derek sees Kevin dancing with his girlfriend, he grabs Kevin's jacket and pulls him off the dance floor. Kevin landed on a table laden with drinks and cut his hand slightly on one of the glasses which broke. Here the appropriate offences are battery and ABH. The word 'slightly' clearly shows that neither **s 20** nor **s 18** is relevant, so no marks will be gained for discussing these. Grabbing someone's coat will be a battery, as touching a person's clothes can amount to the application of unlawful force, as stated in **Thomas**. If the battery causes harm the appropriate charge will be ABH under **s 47** which is an assault occasioning actual bodily harm. A cut, even if slight, is likely to be seen as ABH as it is more than trivial, as required by **Chan-Fook**. The main issue regarding **s 47** is one of causation. Both **Roberts** and **Savage** are relevant. In **Roberts**, it was held that a foreseeable event would not break the chain of causation between an assault (assault or battery) and any resulting injury. In **Savage,** the throwing of the beer was a battery and the glass breaking was foreseeable, facts which are quite similar to these. It was also confirmed in **Savage** that *mens rea* was only needed for the battery. Here Derek grabbed Kevin's jacket so clearly intended the battery, and the battery caused the harm, so a charge under **s 47** should succeed.

Examination tip

It is **good practice** to be selective. Select only the law that applies to the given facts. This shows that you understand the law well enough to know what is relevant.

It is **bad practice** to write all you know about an area just because you know it well. Even if it is right, you will gain no marks if it is not relevant to the facts given

There is limited time in most exams and examiners rarely set a question which requires you to cover everything. For practice in being selective, complete the following exercise.

Task 7 Clue spotting – application practice

Look at the brief comments taken from problem scenarios and note the appropriate offence and the main issues. Also, note what to avoid discussing because it won't earn you marks. The first one is done for you as an example.

Disgusted with the service Sara picked up her plate and threw the food at the waiter. The plate slipped from her grasp and badly bruised the waiter.

Most appropriate offence: it is likely to be at least battery as she used unlawful force, and probably ABH (a bad bruise was caused).

Issues:

Battery can be indirect – **Haystead**

There is no need to intend or be reckless as to harm for the battery to become ABH – **Savage**

A bad bruise is likely to be seen as more than trivial – **Chan-Fook**

Clearly neither **s 18** nor **s 20** is appropriate so there is no need to discuss these.

Frank climbed onto her wall and stared through the window. She started shaking and later suffered stress and depression.

Mick threw a bicycle at Ben who was pruning his roses, as Ben threw his arms up to defend himself he caught his wife's arm with his pruning knife, causing a deep cut.

In all problem questions, you need to take a logical approach. First, read the facts carefully to ensure that you understand the points raised by the scenario. Then apply the relevant law in a logical manner, using cases in support. All exam questions can be approached in a similar way:

identify the law

state the law (using relevant cases)

apply the law (using relevant cases)

reach a conclusion (based on your application)

Task 8 Application practice

As practice for an exam question, try this with the case of **Ireland**. Read the facts of the case and then use your knowledge of the *actus reus* and *mens rea* of the non-fatal offences to apply the law to these facts. Use the following as a guide.

Identify the law (which is the most appropriate offence or offences?)

State the law: define the appropriate offence(s) (all parts of the AR and MR)

***Actus reus:* Explain all parts of the AR using appropriate case(s) in support. Most of these offences are result crimes, so causation can be important, but only discuss this if relevant**

Apply this law to the facts

***Mens rea:* Explain the MR for the particular offence using appropriate case(s) in support**

Apply the rules on intent and/or subjective recklessness to the facts

Reach a conclusion based on your application

Essay questions (evaluation)

The 'Essay pointers' and 'Key criticisms' are intended to provide you with information to use in an essay where you have to evaluate a given area of law. Look through these (and your answer to Task 6) before doing the evaluation practice below.

This is an example of a typical exam question taken from the AQA paper June 2012 and worth 25 marks.

Consider what criticisms may be made of the non-fatal offences against the person. Discuss what reforms might be introduced to deal with these criticisms.

Again, a logical approach is needed. You should:

State what the current law is

Identify and explain where it is unsatisfactory

Support your comments with cases and/or examples

Discuss where reforms are needed including any that have been proposed or implemented

The following exercise will give you a basis for such a discussion.

Task 9 Evaluation practice

Look at the three brief comments below and then:

State what the current law is, using cases as appropriate

Expand on the statement (this can be for or against it or just a brief comment of your own)

Support your comments with cases and/or examples

If reforms have been implemented or proposed, add these

> *For s 47, it seems harsh that no* mens rea *is required for the harm caused*
>
> *S 47 and s 20 carry the same sentencing maximum but they are very different offences*
>
> *Assault and battery are not included in the Offences Against the Person Act but are developed through common law*

There is no 'right' answer to evaluation questions, opinions vary and you can form your own – but **always** use cases and/or examples to back up what you say.

Task 10 Examination practice: evaluation

Try the above exam question using the notes you made for Tasks 6 and 9. Here is the question again:

> *Consider what criticisms may be made of the non-fatal offences against the person. Discuss what reforms might be introduced to deal with these criticisms.*

Answers to self-test questions and tasks

Applying the rules on intent and recklessness to battery, the prosecution must prove the following:

for direct intent, that it was D's aim or purpose to apply unlawful force

for indirect intent, that the application of force was a virtual certainty and D appreciated this

for recklessness, that D recognises a risk that unlawful force will be applied and goes ahead and takes that risk

Self-test questions Chapter 2 Assault and battery

The current definition of assault is to cause someone to apprehend immediate and unlawful personal violence.

Words alone can constitute an assault as shown in **Wilson**.

The *mens rea* for assault is intention or recklessness (to cause someone to apprehend immediate and unlawful personal violence).

A battery does not have to be hostile as seen in **Thomas**.

Consent and self-defence may make a battery lawful.

Task 2

In **Roberts**, the action by the victim did not break the chain of causation because it was foreseeable. The type of action which might do so is 'something daft', as was decided by the CA in **Williams & Davis**.

Self-test questions Chapter 3 ABH

This quote came from Swinton LJ in **Ireland**.

The three parts to the *actus reus* are:

assault – the conduct, an assault or battery

occasioning – a matter of causation

actual bodily harm – the consequence

Mens rea is needed for the conduct (assault) only.

The court in **Ireland** relied on **Chan-Fook**.

The HL finally confirmed that the principle in **Roberts** was correct in **Savage and Parmenter**.

Self-test questions Chapter 3 GBH and wounding

'Wound' has been interpreted as any puncture of the skin.

'Grievous bodily harm' has been interpreted as serious harm.

The cases which support the answers to the above two questions are **C v Eisenhower** and **Saunders**.

The difference in the *mens rea* between **s 20 and s 18** is that for **s 20** it is intent or subjective recklessness as to some harm and for **s 18**, it is intent (only) as to serious harm.

The maximum sentences for **s 20** and **s 18** respectively are 5 years and life.

Task 3

Smith was charged with assault occasioning actual bodily harm

Common assault, specifically battery, might have been more successful. This is because he held her down and cut her hair, and even touching her clothes would have been enough according to **Thomas**.

Judge P held cutting hair to be 'bodily' harm because hair was part of the body and was attached to it.

It was decided in **Miller 1954** that 'actual bodily harm includes any hurt or injury that interferes with the health or comfort of the victim'.

That trivial harm does not amount to ABH was decided in **Chan-Fook**.

They followed **Chan-Fook** where 'mere distress' was held to be insufficient for ABH.

Which decision was right is a matter of opinion. The trial court didn't think it was actual bodily harm because she suffered no harm, either physical or psychological. The QBD allowed the appeal because they decided that hair was part of the body. This is true enough but it is still hard to see how it amounts to bodily 'harm', so I prefer the Magistrates' court decision – but you may disagree.

Task 4

Assault can be by silence	Ireland/Constanza
Words may negate an assault	Turbeville v Savage
Immediate is interpreted widely	Smith v Woking
Battery can be indirect	Haystead/DPP v K
Battery can include touching someone's clothing	Thomas
Everyday social contact (e.g., jostling in a queue, a tap on the shoulder) will not amount to a battery because there is implied consent to such actions	Collins v Wilcock
ABH can include psychiatric harm as long as this is more than mere emotions	Chan-Fook
ABH can include cutting someone's hair without consent	DPP v Ross Smith
Occasioning is a matter of causation so if D causes the harm that is enough even if neither intended nor done recklessly	Roberts or Savage
GBH can include psychiatric harm if it is serious	Burstow
GBH can include less serious harm in the case of a child	Bollom

GBH can include the transmission of disease if intentional	**Dica**
A wound requires both layers of the skin to be cut	**Eisenhower**
S 18 includes intent to resist or prevent a lawful arrest and where this is the case the MR as regards the harm is lower. It is enough that D is reckless	**Morrison**

Task 5

ABH requires a minimum of subjective recklessness. D must recognise the risk of either an assault (putting V in fear of violence) or a battery (applying force to V).

GBH or wounding under **s 20** requires a minimum of subjective recklessness. D must recognise the risk of causing some harm.

GBH or wounding under **s 18** requires a minimum of intent. D must have the aim of seriously injuring V (direct intent, **Mohan**) or appreciate that serious injury is a virtual certainty (indirect intent, **Woollin**).

Task 6

You would not be expected to cover all the problems in the law, as there are a great many in this area, mainly because the law itself is so old and in need of updating. In an examination answer, you should include at least a few points from the list below, or possibly several but in less detail. Either way, in a full question, you would need to expand on them and the relevant cases a little, as you did for the examination evaluation practice. A critique of the law should include any positive developments as well as any proposals for reform where these apply, so the list includes both negative and positive comments. Proposals for reform are mainly from the original Law Commission Report No. 218, with a mention of what is likely to be considered in the new Law Commission project starting in 2014.

Negative points	Positive points and/or proposals for reform
Assault and battery are still not included in statute law but left to judicial reasoning alone	The law can be developed to meet new situations and adapt to technological and social changes. For assault, e.g., mobile phone technology means a telephone call is more likely to cause fear of immediate harm (**Ireland**). As regards ABH psychological harm is now included in (**Chan-Fook**), as is cutting a person's hair (**DPP v Smith**), although this latter case is somewhat controversial itself
The word assault is ambiguous, it means the specific offence of causing someone to apprehend immediate personal violence (Ireland) but also means both an assault and a battery for the purpose of finding an 'assault' which occasions harm for s 47	The Law Commission (Report no. 218) proposed replacing assault and battery with a single new offence of assault but which would include the definitions of assault and battery
The language in the 1861 Act is out-dated and unclear. Words such as 'whosoever', 'occasioning', 'grievous' and 'maliciously' are not in common use today and may anyway have meant something different in 1861 when the Act was written	The project to be started by the Law Commission in 2014 will look at modernising and simplifying the language
The structure of the offences is illogical, as are the section numbers. This is partly because the Act was a consolidated one drawing from several sources but it means that the distinction between the offences is unclear	The project to be started by the Law Commission in 2014 will look at restructuring the offences, perhaps into a kind of hierarchy
It seems harsh that no mens rea is required for the harm caused, only for the assault or battery (Savage)	**S 47:** This is arguably implied in the Act which says an assault occasioning ABH, so once you have an assault all you need to make it a **s 47** offence is that harm results

	The Law Commission proposed replacing **s 47** ABH with an offence of intentional or reckless injury and requiring mens rea for the injury caused
The meaning of 'immediate' in assault (and ABH) is vague	The courts have interpreted immediate widely so that a phone call or stalking can be enough to put V in fear of 'immediate' harm (**Ireland/Constanza/Smith**)
S 47 and s 20: the sentencing maximums seem illogical as both sections carry the same maximum but they are very different offences	The judge can take into account the level of harm as well as the level of intent when sentencing (although cannot go beyond the maximum) The Law Commission will look at this in their 2014 project
The different wording of s 18 and s 20, with 'causing' in the former and 'inflicting' in the latter, is misleading	**S 18** and **s 20**: The uncertainty between 'cause' and 'inflict' has been clarified by the HL in **Ireland** and **Burstow** where both **Salisbury** and **Wilson** were approved The Law Commission will, however, look at this in their 2014 project
S 18 and s 20: Essentially these two sections contain four different offences: reckless GBH, reckless wounding, GBH with intent and wounding with intent, which is confusing	**S 18** and **s 20**: The law has developed so that serious psychological harm is now included in GBH (**Ireland** and **Burstow**) and intentional serious biological harm can also amount to GBH (**Dica**).
S 18 and s 20: A wound can be any cut (Eisenhower) which means that technically a small cut could amount to a wound but these are serious offences	**S 18** and **s 20**: the age of the victim is a relevant factor when deciding on whether the harm is serious enough for GBH (**Bollom**)
S 20: It seems harsh that no *mens rea* is required for serious harm, only for some harm (Mowatt)	The Law Commission proposed replacing **s 20** with 'reckless serious injury' *Mens rea* (recklessness) and requiring *mens rea* for the serious injury caused. Wounding would not be a separate offence but come under **s 18** or **s 20** depending on whether the wound was serious or not and whether it was intended
S 18: It seems harsh that the *mens rea* as regards the harm caused is only recklessness, not intent, when resisting arrest (Morrison)	The Law Commission proposed replacing **s 18** with 'intentional serious injury' and removing the part on resisting arrest. Wounding would be as above

39

Task 7 Examination practice – Application

Identify the law; define the appropriate offence.

As she suffered psychiatric illness, the appropriate offence is an assault occasioning actual bodily harm (ABH) under **s 47** of the **Offences against the Person Act (OAPA)**.

Actus reus (AR)

The AR of this offence first requires an assault which must then cause some actual bodily harm. Assault is putting someone in fear of unlawful violence. As V had suffered psychiatric illness, it is likely that she was afraid. It was held in several cases, e.g., **Smith v Woking**, that words, or even silence, can amount to assault. D has therefore committed an assault which is the first step in establishing ABH. There seems to be no issue with causation as his actions in making the silent telephone calls directly caused her illness. Harm is not defined in the Act but psychiatric harm was said to amount to ABH in **Chan-Fook** as long as it is not trivial, so this part of the *actus reus* is also satisfied. We have an assault which caused actual bodily harm, so all parts of the AR are satisfied.

Mens rea (MR)

As regards MR, this is only needed for the assault. This was stated in **Roberts** and confirmed by the HL in **Savage**. D only needs to have intended or been reckless as to putting her in fear of violence; he need not intend any harm. Recklessness is easier to establish than intent and this will suffice. It only needs to be shown that he recognised the risk of putting her in fear but went ahead with his actions (the test for subjective recklessness established in **Cunningham**). In making silent calls to women, it would be likely that he would at least recognise the risk of causing fear and so had **Cunningham** recklessness. MR is also satisfied, so in conclusion he will be guilty of ABH.

There is a possible alternative of inflicting grievous bodily harm (GBH) if the psychiatric illness is serious, as in **Burstow**. This offence comes under **s 20** of the **OAPA**. It does not require a prior assault (**Wilson**). After some doubt this was confirmed in **Dica**. The case of **Saunders** established that GBH meant serious harm (in **Smith** it had been said it must be really serious but this is no longer the case). The MR of the offence is intent or recklessness as to some harm; he need not intend serious harm. If a charge is brought under **s 20** but the harm is not found to be sufficiently serious then the jury can bring in the alternative verdict under **s 47**. This was confirmed in **Savage**. It may anyway be hard to prove MR for **s 20**, as there is no evidence he intended to cause any harm.

In conclusion, there is a possibility of a charge under either **s 20** or **s 47** but the latter is more likely to succeed.

Task 8 Clue spotting – Application practice

Frank climbed onto her wall and stared through the window. She started shaking and later suffered stress and depression.

Most appropriate offence: it is likely to be at least assault and probably ABH.

>   Issues: assault can be by silence **Ireland/Smith v Woking**.
>   ABH includes psychiatric harm – **Chan-Fook**.
>   There is no need to intend or be reckless as to harm for it to be ABH – **Savage.**

There is clearly neither a battery nor **s 18**, so there is no need to discuss these. There is a possible argument for **s 20** if the depression or stress was serious – **Burstow.**

Mick threw a bicycle at Ben who was pruning his roses, as Ben threw his arms up to defend himself he caught his wife's arm with his pruning knife, causing a deep cut.

Most appropriate offence: wounding **s 20**

Issues:

> Wounding requires both layers of the skin to be broken – **Eisenhower** – and Ben's wife had a 'deep cut'
>
> Transferred malice – **Latimer**, – Mick's MR can be transferred from Ben to his wife
>
> Causation: The actions of Ben are foreseeable so will not break the chain of causation – **Roberts**
>
> No need to intend or be reckless as to serious harm for **s 20** – **Mowatt**

Possibly **s 18** if Mick intended serious harm (**Parmenter**)

Clearly not **s 47** ABH as it is a 'deep cut' so there is no need to discuss this. No assault or battery is needed for either **s 18** or **s 20**, so leave these out too when discussing the deep cut.

There is also a possible assault on Ben. He was in fear of violence as he 'threw his arms up to defend himself', but always be sure to read the question carefully to see whether you need to discuss more than one incident.

Task 9 Examination practice – evaluation

For s 47, it seems harsh that no **mens rea** *is required for the harm caused*

The current law is that someone can be guilty of ABH without intending any harm. I believe that the law should be clearer so that the AR and MR match. That no MR is needed for the harm is arguably implied in the Act, because s 47 says an 'assault occasioning ABH', which indicates that you only need an assault and harm caused by that assault to make it an offence. However not only should it be clearer but it is to an extent unjust. In **Savage**, she only intended to throw beer at the other girl, but her conviction was for ABH. This does seem harsh. Also in **Roberts**, he only had intent as regards the battery, but again the conviction was for ABH because she hurt herself jumping out of the car. Although these results may seem harsh, if someone assaults another person perhaps it is right that they should be liable for any injury that results from their actions. Overall, I think it would be better if the offence of ABH required *mens rea* for some kind of harm. The Law Commission has proposed replacing s 47 ABH with an offence of intentional or reckless injury and requiring *mens rea* for the injury caused. I feel these proposals should be implemented but it is many years since the LC report and nothing has yet been done. It is to be hoped that their new project starting in 2014 will have more success.

S 47 and s 20 carry the same sentencing maximum but they are very different offences

The current law is that both s 47 ABH and s 20 GBH or wounding carry a maximum sentence of five years. The fact that both sections carry the same sentencing maximums seems illogical. Not only are they different offences in different sections of the Act, but also the offence of GBH under s 20 is much more serious than s 47, so why would the sentencing be the same? It is true that this is only a recommended maximum but it is still illogical. It may be argued that the judge can take into account the level of harm when sentencing, but the court cannot go beyond the maximum. This means that there could be a serious level of harm for s 20 with only a five-year sentence, but a lower level of harm which only amounted to ABH could carry the same sentence because of the circumstances.

The judge can also take into account the level of intent when sentencing, but as s 20 as well as s 47 can be committed recklessly, the result may still be illogical. It would be better if there were clear guidelines as to what amount of harm justifies a particular sentence and this should be different for each section. The Law Commission refers to the lack of a clear hierarchy in the introduction to their 2014 project, specifically noting that there is no clear hierarchy of offences and that s 20 is seen as more serious than s 47 but has the same maximum sentence. The Law Commission proposed a maximum of 5 years for s 47, as now, but a maximum 7 years for s 20. This seems more realistic, but the reforms were suggested back in 1998 and although a new project is underway, any changes may be a long way off becoming reality.

Assault and battery are not included in the Offences against the Person Act but are developed through common law

The current law is that assault is a common law offence which covers the two separate offences of an assault or a battery. The fact that assault and battery are not included in the **Offences against the Person Act** is a bad thing in one way, because it would be better if the law on all these offences were to be in one place. However, one positive thing about the offences not being in an Act is that they can be developed through common law by judges. Whilst Parliament is supreme and is elected, so that law made through an Act of Parliament is preferable, there are advantages to judge-made law. Situations like that in **Ireland**, where someone was put in fear by D making telephone calls, would probably not have been covered by the Act even if assault were in it. This is because mobile communications were not possible at that time. With mobile phone technology, people may be afraid of 'immediate' violence because the person using the phone could be nearby. In **Ireland**, the CA said, "*We must apply the law to the conditions as they are in the 20th century*". This shows that judges can adapt to changing situations and advances in technology as they happen and not wait for Parliament to amend the Act. In addition, the fact that the courts have amended the law to include words as well as gestures in assault is an improvement. As Lord Steyn said (also in **Ireland**) "*The proposition that a gesture may amount to an assault, but that words can never suffice, is unrealistic and indefensible*". The Law Commission recommended that assault should be defined as 'intentionally or recklessly causing another to believe force is imminent'. This would cover the situations above as it would include words, gestures or silence and 'imminent' is wider than 'immediate'. In conclusion, I feel that the Act should be replaced so that the definition is wide enough to cover such situations but the law will have been made by Parliament rather than judges. The Law Commission started a new project in 2014 so it is to be hoped that more notice will be taken of their recommendations this time.

Task 10 Examination question

For how to answer this question look at the points made in the table in Task 6, and also look at the answers for Task 9. For an examination question, you would need to do this for a few more of the points raised. You would then need a conclusion which ties in to the question. This could be along the lines of:

In conclusion, it can be seen that there are a great many criticisms which may be made of the law on the non-fatal offences against the person. Although judges have made some attempt at addressing a few of these there is a limited amount that can be done without a major re-structuring of the Act. It is to be hoped that after so many years the new Law Commission project will receive some parliamentary time, so that the suggested reforms noted above can be introduced to deal with the remaining problems.

The following abbreviations are commonly used. You may use them in an examination answer, but write them in full the first time, e.g., write 'actual bodily harm (ABH)' and thereafter that you can just write 'ABH'.

General

Draft Code – A Criminal Code for England and Wales (Law Commission No. 177), 1989

CCRC Criminal Cases Review Commission

ABH actual bodily harm

GBH grievous bodily harm

D defendant

C claimant

V Victim

CA Court of Appeal

HL House of Lords

SC Supreme Court

Acts

S – section (thus **s 1** Theft Act 1968 refers to section 1 of that Act)

s 1(2) means section 1 subsection 2 of an Act

OAPA – Offences against the Person Act 1861

In cases – these don't need to be written in full

CC (at beginning) chief constable

CC (at end) county council

BC borough council

DC district council

LBC London borough council

AHA Area Health Authority

J Justice

LJ Lord Justice

LCJ Lord Chief Justice

LC Lord Chancellor

AG Attorney General

CPS Crown Prosecution Service

DPP Director of Public Prosecutions

AG Attorney General

www.ingramcontent.com/pod-product-compliance
Lightning Source LLC
Chambersburg PA
CBHW051259170526
45165CB00004B/1774